# Free to Grow

## *Overcoming Setbacks and Disappointments*
### Group Member's Guide

By: Jimmy Ray Lee, D.Min.

Communications should be addressed to:
Living Free Ministries, Inc.
P. O. Box 22127
Chattanooga, TN 37422-2127
Phone: 1-800-879-4770
Email: info@livingfree.org

Unless otherwise identified, Scripture quotations in this volume are from the Holy Bible, New International Version ® Copyright ©1973, 1978, 1984, International Bible Society. Used by permission of Zondervan Bible Publishers. Other Scripture quotations marked KJV are from the King James Version of the Bible. Those identified TLB are from The Living Bible, and those identified PHILLIPS are from the New Testament in Modern English, J. B. Phillips, translator. The Scripture quotations marked THE MESSAGE are taken from The Message, copyright © 1993, 1994, 1995, 1996, 2000, 2001, 2002. Used by permission of NavPress Publishing Group.

©Living Free Ministries, 2006. All rights reserved.

All rights are reserved. No part of the material protected by this copyright notice may be reproduced or utilized in any form or by any means, electronic or mechanical, including photocopying, recording, or any information storage and retrieval system, without written permission from the Living Free Ministries.

ISBN 10: 1-58119-077-8
ISBN 13: 978-1-58119-077-9

Layout: Louise Lee
Cover Photo: www.comstock.com

### About the Author

Dr. Jimmy Ray Lee is the founder and president emeritus of Living Free, Inc. He is the author of *Understanding the Times* and several small group studies published by Living Free, Inc. Under the direction and guidance of Dr. Lee, Living Free, Inc. produced Living Free—a high impact, video-based training. This training helps churches develop Christ-centered small groups that deal with the contemporary problems that people face today.

Dr. Lee is the founder and honorary chairman of Project 714 (now known as National Center for Youth Issues), a chemical prevention/intervention program for schools. He also founded an inner-city ministry called Ark Ministries that reached 600 to 700 young people weekly. He started the Chattanooga Teen Challenge and served as its president for three years. Jimmy served as Nashville Teen Challenge executive director during its formative years.

In 1983 he was awarded the "Service to Mankind Award" presented by the Highland Sertoma Club in Hixson, Tennessee.

# Free to Grow

## Overcoming Setbacks and Disappointments

### Contents

|  | Page |
|---|---|
| Preface | 3 |
| Session 1 — Who Am I? | 4 |
| Session 2 — Unmasked Faces | 8 |
| Session 3 — Facing the Truth of Disappointments | 13 |
| Session 4 — Forgive as God Forgave You | 19 |
| Session 5 — Setting Boundaries | 24 |
| Session 6 — Childlike Versus Childish | 30 |
| Session 7 — Making Choices | 36 |
| Session 8 — Freedom and Responsibility | 41 |
| Session 9 — Fresh Start | 46 |
| Session 10 — Developing the Character of Christ | 51 |
| Session 11 — Developing Freedom in Christ | 57 |
| Session 12 — Developing a Future in Christ | 62 |
| A Plan of Salvation | 70 |
| References | 71 |

Group Member's Guide: *Free to Grow*, Living Free, P. O. Box 22127, Chattanooga, TN 37422-2127

# Preface
## To The Free to Grow Group

Welcome to *Free to Grow*. The purpose of this group is to help participants be free of hindrances or setbacks that have arrested or are presently hindering their spiritual development. Our lives are shaped by our experiences in early life, ages birth through age 12. Our emotional and spiritual development is often hindered by rejection, which comes in many forms.

In the healing process, we believe it is vital that Christ be the center of our life and that we build relationships around us with people who care about and pray for us regularly. Anchoring God's Word into our daily living will provide hope and direction. Our hope is that each participant will acknowledge the hurt but not wallow in or nurse (hold on to) the past. Our goal is to go forward in each session, treating *Free to Grow* as a 12-week journey toward wholeness in Christ.

Although we believe that all of us are created in God's image and consist of a body, soul, and spirit, our approach is primarily spiritual and biblical rather than psychological or physiological. As noncredentialed persons, we promise no professional psychological expertise. However, we do have a desire to see the Lord help the participants with their struggles.

It is important that each person participate from start to finish. This is a journey where each session builds on the previous session.

We suggest that all *Free to Grow* group members complete the *Insight Group* as a prerequisite to this group. Membership in an *Insight Group* prior to the *Free to Grow* group helps to prepare the participants for this group. Even though they may want to learn how to live a life free to grow, participation in an *Insight Group* helps them begin the process by looking at themselves first.

> *. . . we believe it is vital that Christ be the center of our life and that we build relationships around us with people who care about and pray for us regularly.*

The group should meet each week for one hour and fifteen minutes, but more time may be planned if necessary. The material is designed for twelve sessions. Some resource materials that would be helpful are *Small Group Skills Guide*, *Understanding the Times and Knowing What to Do* and the *Living Free* video training. These publications are available from Living Free Ministries on the web at LivingFree.org. We also recommend two books that will be helpful in understanding the setbacks and disappointments people face. The books are *Broken Children, Grown Up Pain* by Paul Hegstrom and *Hurt People Hurt People* by Sandra D. Wilson.

It is important to note that the *Free to Grow* group is not a substitute for medical or psychological care. Participants should not be advised

At the conclusion of the course, check into opportunities to join another Living Free support group.

It is our prayer that through participating in and completing this study, you will have a greater understanding of the freedom you have in Christ.

Please be faithful in your attendance at each group meeting and do the assignments in your group member guide before each group session.

As you and the small group walk together through this study, may you discover complete freedom to grow in Christ.

I want to thank Mark Caldwell and Dr. Steve Bradshaw for the encouragement and advice they provided to me while writing this material. They were a source of strength.

# Session 1 — Who Am I?

**Personal Preparation: Getting Ready for Session One**

## Welcome

**Personal Notes**

Welcome to *Free to Grow*. You have taken a positive step. We thank God for your participation.

During this course, there will be suggested time alone with God in meditation, prayer, and scripture reading. This time with God is vital to being *Free to Grow*. We encourage you to be faithful in your devotion time with the Lord.

For this session, read Genesis 1.

*Personal notes (handwritten):*
- Diane
- Brenda
- Elizabeth
- Jazmine (cardiologist)
- Robin's Mom Sherry
- Brenda's son (eye)
- Shawna
- Becca
- Robin
- Amanda

## Self-Awareness

The purpose of this *Free to Grow* group is to help participants to be free of hindrances or setbacks that have arrested or are presently hindering their spiritual growth. We often find that our lives are shaped by our experience in early life, often caused by rejection, which comes in many forms.

In this session, we will focus on being made in the image of God. After being made in the image of God, our first parents, Adam and Eve, distorted our resemblance to God. However, God sent His son, Jesus Christ, to redeem us from the fall of man—"Therefore, just as sin entered the world through one man, and death through sin, and in this way death came to all men, because all sinned...For if the many died by the trespass of one man, how much more did God's grace and the gift that came by the grace of the one man, Jesus Christ, overflow to the many!" (Romans 5:12,15).

Session 1 — Group Member's Guide: *Free to Grow*, Living Free, P. O. Box 22127, Chattanooga, TN 37422-2127

In this session we will focus on the godlike qualities in man—both being a person. "To sum up, God is an independent person with the capacity to long, think, choose, and feel. A human being is a dependent person with the same four capacities" (Crabb, p. 96).

Edward T. Welch in *The Journal of Biblical Counseling* (p. 29) states:

> Articulated most clearly in his books *Understanding People* and *Inside Out*, [Larry] Crabb indicates that the image of God in man has to do with what is similar between man and God. What is similar, Crabb suggests, is that God is a person and we too are persons. To be a person means that we have deep longings for relationships: "We all long for what God designed us to enjoy: tension-free relationships filled with deep, loving acceptance and with opportunities to make a difference to someone else" (*Inside Out*, p. 53 ff).

Describe your need for relationships.

Do you feel a vacuum in your heart for a relationship with God? If so, describe.

We often give attention to the image of people rather than the image of God. I have been blessed to have a father who has reflected godly character through his relationships with God and people. He has given his life pastoring small congregations and ministering to the poor and needy with consistency and godliness. Regardless of the circumstances, he has remained the same over the years. As I get older, I see more and more of the image of God in my father. It has been there all the time, but I see it better now. When I think about God, I think about my father, yet my father would not meet the world's standards of success. However, I believe he will have a "front row seat in heaven."

What person(s) has impacted your life the most in a positive way? *Pastor & Mrs. Howlett, Mom, Dad*

Every human being has worth in God's eyes. Also included are the poor and needy. What does Proverbs 14:31 say about those who oppress the poor?

What does this verse say about those who are kind to the needy?

All mankind—both rich and poor—is made in the image of God. Made in the image of God, we have the ability to make moral choices, grow spiritually, love God, and grow in righteousness.

# Spiritual-Awareness

To be like God means to be like Christ. Christ is the image of the invisible God. Being Christlike enables us to have fellowship with God. However, this does not mean we are gods or can become gods. We are still created beings who are dependent upon God.

Although we were made to resemble God, we are not equal with Him. "To whom will you compare me? Or who is my equal?" (Isaiah 40:25).

*Genesis 1:1-25*
In these verses God describes His work of creation. After looking back on His creation, God made a pronouncement about His work up to that point.

What was His declaration in verse 25?

*Genesis 1:26-27*
Although God was pleased with creation, He still lacked a creature that reflected His own image.

How did He solve this need?

*Genesis 1:31*
With man being a special part of His creation, He once again makes another announcement concerning His creation.

What did He say in this verse?

*Ephesians 4:24*
This verse provides hope that we can advance in our development and be changed into the people God wants us to be.

What do you think this means?

*James 3:9*
With our tongue, we can praise God or curse people.

What does this fact reveal about us ? *Choice*

# Application

Being made in the image of God brings worth and dignity to man. We, as people, have something no other part of creation, including animals and other living creatures, posseses: the image of God.

We are made with a purpose and plan. However, we err so often by depending on our own self-made image. This often leads to dependence upon self and a life of pain and disappointment.

It is wonderful to know that God designed us "to be conformed to the likeness of His Son . . . What, then, shall we say . . . If God is for us, who can be against us?" (Romans 8:29,31).

Write a prayer to God expressing your thanks to Him for being made in His image. Ask Him to help you during the next few weeks of *Free to Grow* to better understand what it means to be made in His image. Also, ask for His help in overcoming setbacks and disappointments you have experienced in your life.

*[handwritten: Comfort / Encouragement]*

*[handwritten: Renew my mind / Part of the body of believers / Uniquely created / Eternally valued / Irreplaceably Significant]*

Memorize Jeremiah 29:11, " 'For I know the plans I have for you,' declares the LORD, 'plans to prosper you and not to harm you, plans to give you hope and a future.' "

Ask God to help you stand on this verse during the next few weeks in the *Free to Grow* group.

As you start *Free to Grow,* there may be major or minor changes or adjustments that need to happen in your life through God's grace. Let's remember the Chinese proverb, "If we don't change our direction, we are apt to end up where we are headed" (Wilson, p. 96).

# Session 2: Unmasked Faces

**Personal Preparation: Getting Ready for Session Two**

## Meet With God

**Personal Notes**

Take 30 minutes each day to be alone with God in meditation and prayer. Read Exodus 34 and 2 Corinthians 3.

In Session 1 we discussed Jeremiah 29:11 as the verse we will stand on during the next few weeks of *Free to Grow*.

*Plans for me*

Describe a situation or thought since our last session that brought this verse to mind.

> "For I know the plans I have for you," declares the LORD, "plans to prosper you and not to harm you, plans to give you hope and a future" (Jeremiah 29:11).

*compassionate*
*gracious*
*slow to anger*
*abounding in love*
*" " faithfulness*
*forgiving*

## Self-Awareness

Most of us wear a mask, whether for short periods of time or continually. By wearing a mask, we can be seen as we desire to be seen. We become performers, acting out a part in specific situations or perhaps for our entire lives.

What are some common masks that people use to conceal their real identity or feelings?

We may even wear a mask that serves as our identity. Masks can be used as hiding places. Bitterness, anger, and sadness are often hidden behind masks; with time, the masks may become hardened.

In Genesis 3:10, Adam said, "I was afraid because I was naked; so I hid." We have been hiding ever since.

Describe a time in your life (present or past) that you hid behind a mask. Why did you feel it was necessary?

One of the greatest blessings in life is understanding that your true identity is in Jesus Christ and then serving Him as your Savior. If you have not received Jesus Christ as your Savior, please see page 70 for instructions.

As we become more transparent with God and others, we will more and more bear a resemblance to Christ. We will find this wonderful relationship grow as we focus on Him and His Word. In doing so, our Bible studies become a time of spiritual enrichment.

The path to true identity (removing the mask) and freedom in Christ is found in *trusting God* versus *pleasing Him*. We may want to please Him so much we may find ourselves falling prey to the bondage of self-performance. To please God, we must first trust Him and then place our lives and our loved ones in His care.

Hebrews 11:6 declares, "And without faith [trust] it is impossible to please God."

"If my motive is trusting God, then my *value* will be living out of who God says I am, and my *action* will be standing with God, with my sin in front of us, working on it together" (Thrall, McNicol, and Lynch, p. 93).

##  Spiritual-Awareness

Faces portray various expressions. God's face and His presence tend to uncover our hiding places. After Adam and Eve sinned, they "hid from the LORD God among the trees of the garden" (Genesis 3:8).

Let's now look at the importance of our true identity being in Christ. Because of His finished work on the cross, we no longer need masks to cover up our sin or disappointment because "your [our] life is now hidden with Christ in God" (Colossians 3:3).

*Exodus 34:29-30*
When Moses came down from Mount Sinai, he was not aware of how his faced looked.

How does the Bible describe his face after he had spoken with the Lord? **Radiant**

How did Aaron and all the Israelites respond when they saw Moses' face? **afraid to come near him**

Why do you think they responded this way?

---

*Exodus 34:33*
What did Moses do when he finished speaking to the Israelites? **veil on his face**

---

*Exodus 34:34-35*
When Moses entered the Lord's presence, "he removed the veil until he came out" (v 34).

When he came out to tell the Israelites what the Lord had commanded, what did they notice about his face? **radiance**

In summary, when Moses was in the presence of the Lord, his face was radiant; however, when he went before the people he would "put the veil back over his face until he went in to speak with the LORD" (v 35). "Moses' face shined with the 'glory' of having seen the face of God, but the people could not stand to gaze upon the face of Moses" (Icenogle, p. 69).

We are blessed to live under the glory of the new covenant.

---

*2 Corinthians 3:7-11*
Describe the contrast between the old covenant and new covenant, particularly in verses 10 and 11.

---

*2 Corinthians 3:12-17*
How is the veil that dulls the mind removed?

How is it possible for us, under the new covenant, to remove the veil, the mask that we may be wearing as a hiding place?

"The Lord is the Spirit, and where the Spirit of the Lord is" (v 17), there is something special for all of us.

What is it?

Because we are "in Christ," we are *free to grow*.

*2 Corinthians 3:18*
In view of 2 Corinthians 3:7-18, what happens when believers, whose identity is in Christ, live this Christian life with unveiled faces (without masks)?

*God (Holy Spirit with us) gives freedom. We reflect His glory (to be conformed to Jesus' likeness). Romans 8:29*

In Session 1, we discussed who we are based on Genesis 1:27: "So God created man in his own image [or likeness], in the image of God he created him."

Notice in 2 Corinthians 3:18, we are "being transformed into his likeness with ever-increasing glory, which comes from the Lord."

As we dwell in the presence of God by aligning ourselves with God's Word and through prayer and face-to-face community, we will be strengthened in our identity in Him and the glory of the Lord will be seen in our lives.

> As the believer contemplates Jesus through prayer and the reading of the Word, the Spirit of the Lord changes (Greek, *metamorphoumetha*, cf. English, metamorphosis) him into the likeness and appearance he beholds. He is transformed (Romans 12:2 where the same Greek verb appears) into that image from one glorious level to another. The complete likeness to Jesus will come when he sees Him face-to-face (1 John 3:2) (Harris, p. 535).

## Application

By accepting our identity in Christ, we can overcome setbacks, disappointments, and other issues that may have arrested our growth in Him.

Next, we must by faith in Christ (trusting Him) ask Him to help us apply the time-proven biblical principles of living our lives in freedom through Him.

Psalm 8 describes the majesty of our Lord and how He is mindful of us (He comes to us) and cares for us. In verses 5-8, David expresses a truth that we must let develop in our hearts. In verse 5 he says, "You made him [man] a little lower than the heavenly beings and crowned him with glory and honor."

What does it mean to you that you are crowned with glory and honor?

How could this change your attitudes and actions in difficult situations?

David points out that we were made "a little lower than the heavenly beings" (v 5). He did not say "a little higher than the animal kingdom." The lesson here is to look up to Jesus, not down.

> It is . . . humanity's special privilege and duty to look upward to the angels (and beyond the angels to God, in whose image men and women have been made), rather than downward to the beasts. The result is that they become increasingly like God rather than increasingly beast-like in their behavior (Boice, p. 71).

Describe an area in your life in which you are needing help from the Lord to remove a veil from your face and heart that may be hindering your freedom in Christ.

In what ways will you practice looking up to Jesus rather than looking down this week?

Those who face the Son find the shadows of life fall behind them.

# Session 3: Facing the Truth of Disappointments

**Personal Preparation: Getting Ready for Session Three**

 **Meet With God**

Take 30 minutes each day to be alone with God in meditation and prayer. Read 2 Samuel 13-18, Genesis 37 and Genesis 39-45.

**Personal Notes**

*David's son Absalom*

Psalm 32:10 is a verse we can stand on as we face our disappointments: "The LORD's unfailing love surrounds the man [or woman] who trusts in him."

Describe how you picture this verse.

 **Self-Awareness**

It has been said that everyone's wound is different. Each one's wound is his own. Although we may not fully understand each other's disappointments or setbacks in life, we can respect each other's feelings.

One man's story of being set free to grow:

> As I was growing up, I was filled with anger. It lived inside me all the time—and was vented on everyone and everything. Even after I was saved as a teenager and later became a pastor, that anger was present. Through the years, I asked myself, "Why? Why am I so angry?" I could never find the answer—and the anger continued to control my life.
>
> In 1992 I was participating in a *Living Free* training and attended a group. The leader asked the question: "What is the first memory you have of Jesus?"
>
> As I closed my eyes and tried to remember, suddenly the memories flooded my mind. When I was nine years old, my mother was expecting a baby. My younger sister and I were so excited. We were going to have a brother! And then when she was six months along, my mother lost the baby. My father took me to visit her in the hospital. She and I wept together. She tried to comfort me by telling me that the Bible says that if we want to follow Jesus, we have to carry a cross every day. I looked up to see a

Group Member's Guide: *Free to Grow*, Living Free, P. O. Box 22127, Chattanooga, TN 37422-2127

Session 3

minister standing near her bedside confirming her words. Misunderstanding their message, my young mind concluded, "Jesus killed my brother."

Suddenly I understood—I had been angry at Jesus all these years! That realization opened the door to freedom. The group prayed for me. God touched my life and healed me. I was able to let go of the past, to accept God's forgiveness. I was at last free to grow into the person He had designed me to be. (Personal testimony of a participant at the Living Free Conference in October 2005.)

We are finding that our lives are often shaped by our experiences in early life, from birth through age 12.

The wounds of our childhood hinder our emotional development. We grow physically and chronologically yet remain like children, holding on to our fears and rejection. In adulthood, this dynamic makes us feel as if we're crazy, stupid, or defective (Hegstrom, p. 15).

This is often referred to as *arrested development*. Children often develop survival skills that halt their emotional development. Blinded by their pain, they struggle in understanding the love of their heavenly Father for them.

Because of limited cognitive development and skills, children are often prevented from making good decisions and choices. Paul Hegstrom notes, "Five traumas will generally arrest normal development in a prepubescent child: rejection (neglect), incest, molestation, emotional abuse, and physical abuse" (p. 24). However, rejection (real or emotional abandonment) seems to be the most damaging to the child. "Early emotional experiences knit long-lasting patterns into the very fabric of the brains's neural networks" (Lewis, Amini, and Lannon, p. 176). The hurt boy becomes the angry man.

Without identifying specific persons, describe a time of rejection in your prepubescent life (birth-12 years old) that has been a stumbling block for you. (Please note this does not mean that we are to force memories. If nothing is there, that is fine.)

If you do not feel comfortable sharing with the group, then share with a person whom you trust (one-on-one) as the Holy Spirit leads you.

In order to begin the healing process, we need to recognize and admit the problem that was the source of our rejection or trauma.

Remaining a victim is not the answer. To be serious about our healing, we must accept responsibility (whether great or small) and stop blaming others for our problems.

When we refuse to nurse (hold on to) or curse (be angry about) the past, we have opened the door for a fresh life in Christ. Are you ready for the fresh life in Christ? Describe.

Childhood trauma and rejection often hinder our spiritual and emotional growth. Adult characteristics of arrested development include uncontrollable anger, isolation, barriers (self-protective techniques learned in childhood), self-hatred, low self-esteem, and self-doubt. Since children have leaned to internalize this pain, they carry it into adulthood, accepting it as normal behavior. They learn the three childhood rules—<u>don't talk, don't trust, don't feel.</u>

Without God's help, these characteristics can cause much sorrow in marriage and family relationships.

What does trusting God to heal your pain look like for you?

As we turn to God's Word for direction and hope, we can be assured that <u>His Word is applicable for us today.</u> Psalm 119:89-90 declares this truth.

Describe the assurance in these verses that shows God's Word is applicable to our past (early childhood) as well as to our present life.

*His word <u>endures</u>*
*He is faithful!*

*You care(d) & are (were) with me.*
*You created me.*
*I am loved by you!*

## Spiritual-Awareness

It is comforting to know that with God's help we can face the truth of disappointments in life. "Then you will know the truth, and the truth will set you free" (John 8:32).

The Bible provides examples of people who got stuck in the past and others who moved on and were free to grow.

2 Samuel 14:23-24
It seems that <u>David allowed his official duties to interfere with the needs of his son.</u> This passage points out the distance in their relationship.

Describe this scene in your own words.

*David did not receive Absalom; he sent him to "his own" house.*

2 Samuel 14:25
Describe Absalom's personal appearance.

*very handsome*

What impact might all of the praise he received from others have had on him?

*conceit; want to be noticed*

*2 Samuel 14:28*
It is apparent that Absalom experienced the pain of rejection (neglect) from his father, David, one of the most respected men in the Bible.

This verse speaks of a time that Absalom was absent from his father.

What was the time span? *2 years*

*2 Samuel 14:29*
What was Absalom's request in this verse? *sent to Joab twice to see the King*

What message do you think Absalom received from this absence? *rejection*

*2 Samuel 15:13*
Absalom did not deal properly with his father's rejection. He led a conspiracy against his father.

To what did his cunning tactics lead? *people sided with Absalom*

*2 Samuel 18:5*
In the time prior to Absalom's death, David appeared to shift responsibility to others instead of taking it on himself.

What was David's instruction in this passage? *Be gentle with my son*

Who do you think was wounded more by this rebellion, David or

*2 Samuel 18:33*
Absalom's life ended in tragedy, and David experienced perhaps the saddest day in his life.

Frame this verse with your own words.

God can and will replace pain, from whatever cause, with His love. "Give us gladness in proportion to our former misery! Replace the evil years with good" (Psalm 90:15-16 TLB).

Although we do not have any knowledge of Absalom's childhood, it is obvious that his life was influenced by David's neglect and model as a father. Absalom was born with the capacity to be evil or to be a faithful servant of God. Although his life was probably shaped by poor decisions from a father who loved him, Absalom still had a choice. Unfortunately, he made the wrong choice.

# Application

There is good news. We can overcome the disappointments of life. We will note two examples—Joseph and David.

Joseph experienced rejection when his brothers threw him into a cistern. At the time he was about 17 years old. This appears to be a culmination of sibling rejection and jealousy that had existed for years before this trauma.

Prior to throwing him in the cistern, what did Joseph's brothers do to humiliate him? See Genesis 37:23-24.

In Genesis 37:25-28, the Scriptures record that, "As they sat down to eat their meal, they looked up and saw a caravan of Ishmaelites coming from Gilead . . . his brothers pulled Joseph up out of the cistern and sold him for twenty shekels of silver to the Ishmaelites, who took him to Egypt."

What further rejection do you see Joseph experiencing as his brothers ate their meal during his time of distress?

Have you ever experienced a time of distress when everyone else around you was totally disinterested in your pain? Describe.

How did you respond?

Later Joseph experienced another setback when Potiphar's wife falsely accused him of sexual advances. He was placed in prison; when the chief cupbearer could have helped Joseph, he forgot about him (see Genesis 39-40).

As time went on, God gave Joseph favor, and he was advanced to Pharaoh's top official.

Genesis 50:15-21 provides us with the bottom line. Joseph maintained a good attitude, and in the end he still cared for his brothers. Genesis 50:19-20 shows that even in all of his disappointments and setbacks, he kept his perspective right.

What did he say to his brothers concerning God's perspective on his entire experience of rejection and disappointment?

We read in Romans 8:28, "And we know that in all things God works for the good of those who love him, who have been called according to his purpose."

Write a prayer to God indicating your willingness to let Him work out all the details of your life in His time and in His way.

Now let's look at David. He was not a good role model as a father. He was a murderer, adulterer, and schemer and was neglectful. One of the greatest disappointments of Absalom concerning his father occurred after Amnon raped his sister Tamar. "King David heard the whole story and was enraged, but he didn't discipline Amnon . . . Absalom quit speaking to Amnon—not a word, whether good or bad—because he hated him for violating his sister Tamar (2 Samuel 13:21-22 THE MESSAGE).

However, despite his failures, David was willing to ask God for forgiveness and stay on track with Him. God gave David one of the highest compliments in the entire Bible.

From Acts 13:22, what is God's compliment?

Do you consider yourself a person after God's own heart? Why or why not?

Write a prayer on how you will seek to have a heart similar to the one God saw in David. Describe the repentance issues you might need to discuss with God.

The two prayers in this section will be very important as we start to trust God to remove the obstacles in our lives and replace them with a freshness of His Holy Spirit over the next few weeks in *Free to Grow*.

God has given us a free will. We can overcome disappointments and setbacks in our lives. Romans 12:2 encourages us to change: "Do not conform any longer to the pattern of this world, but be transformed by the renewing of your mind."

# Session 4: Forgive as God Forgave

**Personal Preparation: Getting Ready for Session Four**

 **Meet With God**

**Personal Notes**

Take 30 minutes each day to be alone with God in meditation and prayer. Read Colossians 3, Ephesians 4, and 1 Corinthians 13.

*love*

Let's go back to our theme verse again.

"For I know the plans I have for you," declares the LORD, "plans to prosper you and not to harm you, plans to give you hope and a future" (Jeremiah 29:11).

From this verse, describe briefly a hope you have for the future that you have placed in God's care.

Hope is confident expectation.

*He will be present & help me. I am not to fear.*

# Self-Awareness

While God indeed has plans to prosper us and give us hope for the future, it is possible for us to have things in our lives that can hinder our participation in His plans for us. Unforgiveness and a root of bitterness in our heart are two of those things. However, God has detailed a way for us to overcome these entangling resentments. It is called forgiveness.

Forgiveness is a major step in overcoming disappointments and the setbacks of life. To forgive means to turn loose (or let go), release, or remit. Forgiveness requires our facing the truth. In order to experience true freedom in Christ, we must forgive those who have caused us harm or disappointment. This also includes forgiving ourselves.

What has been your greatest challenge—forgiving yourself or others? Describe.

Forgiveness is an act of God's grace. To give as well as to experience true forgiveness, we are totally dependent on God's grace. Forgiveness can open up a whole new perspective on life.

In what ways will you seek to experience God's grace in overcoming unforgiveness, whether from a past life experience or a present situation?

Dr. Steve Bradshaw of Bryan College in Dayton, Tennessee, often states that things that are buried dead stay buried but things that are buried alive come back to haunt us.

Forgiveness helps us bury things dead. Forgiveness is not forgetting. It is choosing to remember the past in a way that does not affect the present in a toxic way.

*"Not my fault." "Doing their job as they were taught." "Don't blindly trust people or their knowledge. Trust God."*

A special joy comes from God when we are able to forgive. Proverbs 12:20 describes this joy. Who is it for?

*"for those who promote peace"*

Hebrews 12:15 (KJV) describes something called a "root of bitterness." Why do you suppose that resentment and anger toward someone who has wronged and hurt us is described as a "root"?

Session 4 — Group Member's Guide: *Free to Grow*, Living Free, P. O. Box 22127, Chattanooga, TN 37422-2127

# Spiritual-Awareness

Christians are a forgiven people. Forgiven by the Lord, we have both the reason and the responsibility to forgive others. Forgiveness is a *decision* and *choice* we make. It is not based on our feelings but rests clearly on instructions from the Bible.

Although much has been written about the pain of unforgiveness suffered by both believers and nonbelievers, the Bible remains the greatest resource to guide us from unforgiveness to freedom in Christ.

- Our Example for Forgiveness

*Colossians 3:13; Ephesians 4:32*
In what areas are we to offer forgiveness?

*as Christ forgave me*

What did Paul say about our example for forgiveness?

*as Christ*

Christ is our example. We "should follow in his steps" (1 Peter 2:21).

- The Pain of Unforgiveness

*Matthew 18:21-35*
This passage describes the parable of the unmerciful servant.

What did Jesus say about the unforgiving servant in verses 33-35?

*we must forgive from the heart*

- The Road to Reconciliation

Forgiveness can be described as a gift. It is something you give. It is something you receive.

*1 Corinthians 13:5*
Substitute the word *forgiveness* for *love* in this verse.

God's love and true forgiveness are inseparable.

David Augsburger in *The Freedom of Forgiveness* says this about starting the road to forgiveness and reconciliation:

> Yes, forgive immediately, forgive continually, and then forgive—finally . . . end it with finality! . . . You may recall the hurt, but you will not relive it! No constant reviewing, no rehearsing of the old hurt, no going back to sit on the old gravestone where past grievances lie buried" (p. 39).

## Application

Ken Sande in his book *The Peacemaker* describes four promises that can help you tear down the walls that stand between you and your offender.

> I will not dwell on this incident.
> I will not bring up this incident again and use it against you.
> I will not talk to others about this incident.
> I will not let this incident stand between us or hinder our personal relationship (p. 209).

If you are dealing with an offender, someone you need to forgive, write a prayer to God expressing your need for His strength and your willingness to apply these four promises.

*You provide what I need!*

Resentment means to rewind and review again and again and again.

Bitterness is cancer to the soul.

Ken Sande further states that reconciliation should be pursued at three different levels (pp. 220-222).

- **In Thought**

    Practice Philippians 4:8 to replace your negative thoughts. "Finally, brothers, whatever is true, whatever is noble, whatever is right, whatever is pure, whatever is lovely, whatever is admirable—if anything is excellent or praiseworthy—think about such things."

*Not my fault. 73 + over the counter NDT. God with me provides & leads.*

Session 4 — Group Member's Guide: *Free to Grow*, Living Free, P. O. Box 22127, Chattanooga, TN 37422-2127

- **In Word**

    We should speak well of the other person. Draw attention to the offender's strengths.
    "Now instead, you ought to forgive and comfort him, so that he will not be overwhelmed by excessive sorrow" (2 Corinthians 2:7).

- **In Deed**

    Reconciliation requires action.
    "Dear children, let us not love with words or tongue but with actions and in truth" (1 John 3:18).

Write a prayer to God again asking for His strength and then describe your plan to pursue reconciliation with your offender at these three levels.

*Doing what she was taught.*

You may be in a difficult situation where the other party is not willing to reconcile. If this is the case, first make sure you have forgiven in your own heart. Keep yourself ready to pursue complete reconciliation if/when the other person becomes ready.

Second, wait on God's timing for the other party to join in total reconciliation. It may not be safe to be physically reconciled with some people because they have not shown fruit consistent with repentance. Do not try to force it—let God work it out in His timing.

C. S. Lewis said, "Do not waste time bothering whether you 'love' your neighbor; act as if you did. As soon as we do this, we find one of the great secrets. When you are behaving as if you loved someone, you will presently come to love him" (*Mere Christianity*, p. 116).

# Session 5 Setting Boundaries

**Personal Preparation: Getting Ready for Session Five**

## Meet With God

**Personal Notes**

Take 30 minutes each day to be alone with God in meditation and prayer. Read Exodus 20, 1 John 5 and Jude.

Let's go back to a verse that we shared in Session 3: "The LORD's unfailing love surrounds the man [or woman] who trusts in him" (Psalm 32:10).

In view of sessions 3 and 4, describe the love of God that is promised to you in this verse. *Trust Him in disappointments. Forgive. The Lord loves & keeps you.*

How are you doing with your level of trust in Him? *Daily, persevere, ask for guidance & protection, rely on Him to provide strength & wisdom*

## Self-Awareness

Fences make good neighbors because they are boundaries, not barriers. Setting personal boundaries in order to protect our ability to be *free to grow* is vital to becoming all we can be in Christ. You may have come from a childhood and adolescence where there were unreasonable boundaries or no boundaries. Hegstrom says, "The young child learns by boundaries, directives, either positive consequences for obedience or negative consequences for disobedience. The consistency of the training creates a lifelong pattern in the child" (p. 34).

The type of training and boundaries children receive and experience, whether positive or negative, greatly influences their view of God. In *Hurt People Hurt People*, Sandra Wilson says, "Children generally think of God as an exaggerated parent" (p. 76).

*protective, providing, counted on, wise, expectations*

*fruit of the Spirit of God*

What are some of your earliest memories of boundaries set for you by a parent, guardian, teacher, or older brother or sister?

*hear whistle*

The goal of this session is to begin or enhance the process of establishing appropriate boundaries. This will help you protect yourself from situations that might hinder your growth in becoming whole in Christ.

You need to set boundaries to protect and respect your own needs. As you set godly boundaries, you can more clearly see situations or even people who may hinder your growth. In establishing appropriate boundaries, you will develop levels of trust. For example, you may trust a friend to cut your hair but not trust her to baby-sit your children. You may trust a friend in church to baby-sit your child but not accept his unqualified financial guidance. You may sing in the choir with a friend, but your new boundaries will not permit you to be alone with that person.

Describe some steps you may be taking to establish appropriate boundaries. *Time for devotions*

We should watch for triggering devices that can lead to violating our boundaries. We should take inventory of past experiences that caused us to give in to inappropriate decisions or behaviors. Certain music or visual stimulation associated with past inappropriate actions or decisions may contribute to a setback. Appropriate boundaries may require taking a serious look at temptations—who we associate with, the places we go, or what we watch in the media.

Walking within God's boundaries means we must be prayerfully aware of triggering devices and schemes that Satan may use to weaken our boundaries or even cause us to cross our personal boundaries.

In 2 Corinthians 2:10-11, Paul talks about awareness of such devices. How does he address Satan's schemes in this verse?

*forgiven in the presence of Jesus for "your sake"*
*"takes advantage of us;*
*know how he works"*

# Spiritual-Awareness

Living within God's boundaries provides a joy and fulfillment that cannot be found outside of His loving care. David said, "The boundary lines have fallen for me in pleasant places . . . You have made known to me the path of life; you will fill me with joy in your presence" (Psalm 16:6,11). Let's look at God's Word concerning His boundaries.

*In Your presence is fulness of joy! You will show me the path of life.*

- Blessings are in God's boundaries.

*Jude 21 TLB*
According to this verse, where does God's love reach us and bless us?

When should we stay in His boundaries? *always*

*1 John 5:3*
To walk in His boundaries is to follow His commandments. According to this verse, is obeying His commandments an unreasonable task? Describe.

How do we know we love God? *follow & obey Him & His Word*

A better understanding of God's boundaries for our personal life can help us identify other people's attitudes and actions that may not be in our best interest.

- God's boundaries call us to take care of our personal health and emotional state.

*Matthew 11:28-30*
What does Jesus ask the weary and burdened to do in this passage?

*Come to me*
*Take my yoke & learn from me (easy)*
*Light burden*

- We are to respect the boundaries of the weak.

*John 5:6*
Jesus asked a question of a man at the pool of Bethesda that showed He respected his desires. *Do you want to get well?*

What did Jesus say that shows He respected the man's boundaries?

Session 5 — Group Member's Guide: *Free to Grow*, Living Free, P. O. Box 22127, Chattanooga, TN 37422-2127

- The Bible sets many boundaries—all are in our best interest.

*Luke 18:18-26*
When the young rich ruler asked Jesus what he should do to inherit eternal life, Jesus set some boundaries for him.

What were they? *Sell all & give to the poor. Then, follow me*

The young rich ruler's wealth became a stumbling block. Perhaps if he had just been willing to sell everything, he might not have been required to do so. He was unwilling to follow Jesus totally and went away sad when he could have had the joy of living within God's boundaries.

*Psalm 16:4*
What happens to those who violate God's boundaries, "who run after other gods"? *Suffer more & more*

# Application

There is no better example of God's boundaries for us than the Ten Commandments.

> Our society can be described as one without boundaries and guardrails which has resulted in moral decay. People are searching for direction and purpose in a time when murder, divorce, abortion, and immorality are considered by many as normal.... We have replaced the Ten Commandments with human rules (which always change) and principles (Lee, *The Ten Commandments*, p. 1).

When human rules and principles replace the Ten Commandments, the soul is left searching for its foundation.

Group Member's Guide: *Free to Grow*, Living Free, P. O. Box 22127, Chattanooga, TN 37422-2127  Session 5

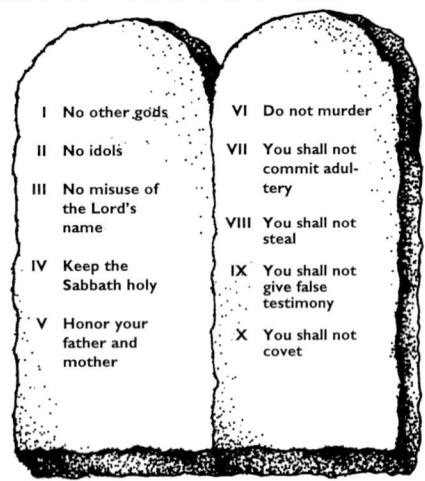

Exodus 20:1-17

Under the new covenant in Christ, the Ten Commandments are written "not on tablets of stone but on tablets of human hearts" (2 Corinthians 3:3). The Holy Spirit helps the believer by giving the person a love for God's law. It is no longer a chore to keep God's laws; we **want** to keep them. Jesus said, "I have not come to abolish them but to fulfill them" (Matthew 5:17) (Lee, *The Ten Commandments*, p. 64).

What did Paul mean when he wrote that in a believer, the Ten Commandments are not written on tablets of stone but on tablets of human hearts? *It's a person's principles to follow & live by*

The Ten Commandments direct us to depend on God's grace.

Describe the commandment(s) that you struggle with most.

Write a prayer to God asking for His help in understanding and setting boundaries. Also, describe actions you can take to better adhere to the commandment(s) and stay in His boundaries.

*Recall His Word; be in awe of Him*
*Gratitude*
*Holy Spirit in me*
*Ask for what I need today*
*Ask for forgiveness & forgive*
*Ask for guidance & protection from evil; Praise Him!*

When you struggle with God's boundaries for your life, remember what Paul says:

> The moment I decide to do good [stay in His boundaries], sin is there to trip me up. I truly delight in God's commands, but it is pretty obvious that not all of me joins in that delight. Parts of me covertly rebel, and just when I least expect it, they take charge.
>
> I've tried everything and nothing helps; I'm at the end of my rope. Is there no one who can do anything for me? Isn't that the real question?
>
> <u>The answer, thank God, is that Jesus Christ can and does.</u> He acted to set things right in this life of contradictions where I want to serve God with all my heart and mind but am pulled by the influence of sin to do something totally different. <u>With the arrival of Jesus, the Messiah, that fateful dilemma is resolved</u>" (Romans 7:21-8:1 THE MESSAGE).

*Jesus*

# Session 6
## Childlike Versus Childish

**Personal Preparation: Getting Ready for Session Six**

## Meet With God

**Personal Notes**

Take 30 minutes each day to be alone with God in meditation and prayer. Read Matthew 18 and 1 Corinthians 13.

Think about the time in your childhood or teenage years that you took on your first responsibility. What was it, and how did you feel about it?

## Self-Awareness

It is important to be childlike in our faith but not be childish in our daily thought life and actions. Being childlike in our faith means to be like children in our dependence on God just as children are dependent on their parent(s). Children seldom worry about tomorrow since they know that they are in the care of loving parent(s).

Since a child's view of God is often developed as a result of the actions of the parent(s), a godly parent is essential for the child's proper spiritual growth.

Although most parents do the best they can, many are not able to provide an example of a godly identity in their own lives. Perhaps you had parents who were inconsistent and confusing in what sort of person they wanted you to be.

Group Member's Guide: *Free to Grow*, Living Free, P. O. Box 22127, Chattanooga, TN 37422-2127

What are some childlike traits that are good examples for us to display as we trust in God?

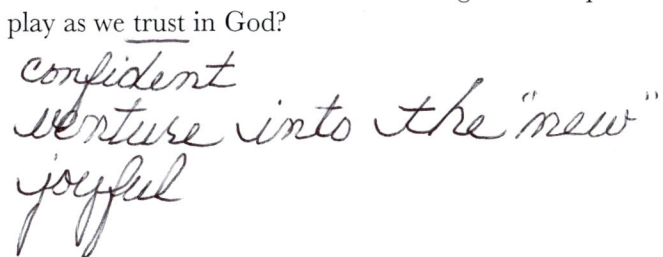

*confident*
*venture into the "new"*
*joyful*

Being childish is entirely different from being childlike. Childish is being silly or foolish. Even adults can be childish—behaving like spoiled brats, never growing up. This is often the case with adults who have not overcome trauma or rejection in their earlier life. Instead of growing into maturity, they are retarded in their emotional and spiritual growth.

In an environment where parents are irresponsible or absent, children often pursue survival skills or pleasure to fill the painful void in their life. The children may grow into adulthood and be fifty-year-olds but still twelve-year-olds in their emotional state. I call them fifty-year-old boys.

While traveling on a busy freeway in Los Angeles, I heard a preacher on the radio describe the difference between a man and a boy.

Boys play house—men build homes.
Boys make babies—men raise families.
Boys demand their rights—men assume responsibility.
Boys look for ways to get out of work—men look for work (Lee, *Understanding the Times*, p. 118).

A childish woman judges a man by his bank account and appearance. A mature but childlike woman looks for character and integrity.

*follows God's direction*

Are there areas in your life where you need to be more responsible and in line with your age and the gifts God has given you? Describe.

God has placed people in the body of Christ (like the members of this small group) to help us grow. Ephesians 4:11-14 describes God-given ministries in the church that prepare us for His plan for our life.

What is the goal for each of us in verse 13?

*each person does work*

Verse 14 gives the results of verse 13. What are they?

*unity*
*unique spiritual gifts*

## Spiritual-Awareness

Let's now look at scriptures that deal with aspects of being childlike versus demonstrating childish behavior.

### Being Childlike

*Matthew 18:3*
What importance does Jesus place on being childlike in this verse?

*to enter heaven*

What do you think He meant by this?

*following our Father, trusting, obedient, part of the family*

*Matthew 18:4*
Who does Jesus refer to as the "greatest in the kingdom of heaven"?

*humble as a little child; dependent, learning*

*Matthew 18:5*
Who do we welcome when we welcome a child? *Jesus*

Jesus' attention is drawn to childlike faith.

---

*Matthew 18:6*
What does Jesus say about those who would cause "one of these little ones who believe in me [Jesus] to sin"? *Better to be drowned*

We can see clearly that children are very important to Jesus. Limited cognitive development prevents children from making good choices. They need to be protected and taught the love of Jesus by word and deed. Otherwise, unless children who experience rejection and trauma receive help, they may grow into adulthood childish in their ways.

---

**Being Childish**

*1 Corinthians 14:20*
Although this verse is in the context of spiritual gifts, it addresses proper thinking and improper (childish) thinking. Describe.

> One does not expect a small child to understand spiritual things. But an adult who is mature in his thinking is willing to seek understanding. On the other hand, children do not develop deep-seated malice or habitual faultfinding. They are quick to forgive and forget. So far as malice is concerned, then we should remain as children, even as babes. But in our thinking and understanding we need to be men (Horton, pp. 228-229). *mature*

*1 Corinthians 3:1-4*
What are indications in these verses that the Corinthian believers needed to grow up? *envy, strife, divisions*

# Application

It is our Lord's desire that we grow into maturity in Him—not blaming parents, friends, circumstances, etc., for our problems. The Apostle Paul writes, "When I was a child, I talked like a child, I thought like a child, I reasoned like a child. When I became a man, I put childish ways behind me" (1 Corinthians 13:11).

In *Putting Away Childish Things*, David Seamands writes:
> Childish things don't simply fall away by themselves as dead leaves fall from a tree. We have to put them away, *katarges* them, and be finished with childish things. The Greek verb *katarges* means to abolish, wipe out, set aside something (Preface).

Putting childish things away is a process requiring a change in our thought life and a willingness to take corrective actions.

Describe any childish thoughts or actions in your life that you need to change (with God's help). *move on, be grateful, ask Him & rely on Him*

What steps do you need to take to grow in this area?
*Daily take time to pray & thank*

Has the process begun? Describe.

Write a prayer to God about your need to change the childish areas in your life and your plans to change—understanding that it is a process to maturity in Christ. Read Philippians 4:8-9 to help you with this prayer.

Meditate on what is true, noble, right (noble), pure, lovely, admirable (good report), excellent (virtue), praiseworthy

God of peace will guard your heart & mind. He will be with me.

Father

His will (in me & community)
daily provision for us, family & friends
forgiveness from & for me
lead us your way; make your will known to us
deliver & keep us from all evil; protect & guide us
You are King, all powerful, & all praise & glory is due & for You!
Thank You... I trust You. I love You. I'm Your Child.

stress (reaction) management & character development strength

Psalm 23

The Lord is my shepherd. Green pastures, quiet waters

1. Is it my problem, or
2. Is it a fact of life? (accept, live with it)

Focus on the tasks He's given me to do.

# Session 7: Making Choices

**Personal Preparation: Getting Ready for Session Seven**

## Meet With God

**Personal Notes**

Take 30 minutes each day to be alone with God in meditation and prayer. Read Deuteronomy 28, Deuteronomy 30, and Acts 7.

In addition to being a famous baseball player, Yogi Berra is known for his unique sayings. He once said, "When you come to a fork in the road, take it."

Have you ever felt that <u>uncertain about a decision you needed to make</u>? Briefly describe.

*Moving, (medical) health*

*Personal Notes (handwritten):*
*Choose His way & life*
*The Word is in your mouth & heart - obey it.*
*Love the Lord*
*Listen to His voice*
*Hold on to Him*

## Self-Awareness

Adam and Eve had a choice in Genesis 3. They made the wrong choice—disobedience—and all of mankind has suffered the consequences. You can choose between obedience and disobedience, but you cannot choose the consequences.

It is because God loves us so much that <u>He gives us freedom to make choices.</u> The freedom of choice goes back to Genesis 2:16-17, "And the LORD God commanded the man, 'You are free to eat from any tree in the garden; but you must not eat from the tree of the knowledge of good and evil, for when you eat of it you will surely die.' "

Although we suffer the consequences of our poor choices, God continues to love us so much that He sent His only Son, Jesus, to pay the price for our sin. Paul points to this good news in Romans 5:8, "But God demonstrates his own love for us in this: While we were still sinners, Christ died for us."

Session 7

Group Member's Guide: *Free to Grow*, Living Free, P. O. Box 22127, Chattanooga, TN 37422-2127

Write a prayer to God about your need to change the childish areas in your life and your plans to change—understanding that it is a process to maturity in Christ. Read Philippians 4:8-9 to help you with this prayer.

*Meditate on what is true, noble, right (noble), pure, lovely, admirable (good report), excellent (virtue), praiseworthy*

*God of peace will guard your heart & mind. He will be with me.*

We must take action to set aside childhood misperceptions and replace them with the instruction in Philippians 4:8-9. The key in this passage is "put into practice." As we practice this biblical principle, we can develop an accurate understanding of God's plan for our lives.

"For it is God who works in you to will and to act according to his good purpose" (Philippians 2:13).

It is our surrender to God and the power of His Spirit within us, not our power, that enables us to "put into practice" the things of Philippians 4:8-9.

*Our tasks to do vs facts of life we aren't to solve. (avoid stress)*

*stress (reaction) management & character development strength*

*Psalm 23*

*The Lord is my shepherd. Green pastures, quiet waters*
1. *Is it my problem, or*
2. *Is it a fact of life? (accept, live with it)*

*Focus on the tasks He's given me to do.*

# Session 7: Making Choices

**Personal Preparation: Getting Ready for Session Seven**

## Meet With God

Take 30 minutes each day to be alone with God in meditation and prayer. Read Deuteronomy 28, Deuteronomy 30, and Acts 7.

In addition to being a famous baseball player, Yogi Berra is known for his unique sayings. He once said, "When you come to a fork in the road, take it."

Have you ever felt that <u>uncertain about a decision you needed to make</u>? Briefly describe.

*Moving, (medical) health*

**Personal Notes**

*Choose His way & life*
*The Word is in your mouth & heart - obey it.*
*Love the Lord*
*Listen to His voice*
*Hold on to Him*

## Self-Awareness

Adam and Eve had a choice in Genesis 3. They made the wrong choice—disobedience—and all of mankind has suffered the consequences. You can choose between obedience and disobedience, but you cannot choose the consequences.

It is because God loves us so much that <u>He gives us freedom to make choices.</u> The freedom of choice goes back to Genesis 2:16-17, "And the LORD God commanded the man, 'You are free to eat from any tree in the garden; but you must not eat from the tree of the knowledge of good and evil, for when you eat of it you will surely die.'"

Although we suffer the consequences of our poor choices, God continues to love us so much that He sent His only Son, Jesus, to pay the price for our sin. Paul points to this good news in Romans 5:8, "But God demonstrates his own love for us in this: While we were still sinners, Christ died for us."

Group Member's Guide: *Free to Grow*, Living Free, P. O. Box 22127, Chattanooga, TN 37422-2127

Within your comfort level, describe a choice you have made in your life that has caused you to suffer negative consequences.

Do you seem to have trouble learning from experience and continue to make poor choices about certain things? If so, what sort of things are these?

"What we live with, we learn, and what we learn, we practice. What we practice we become, and what we become has consequences" (Lawson, p. 17).

New choices will bring along new consequences. Are there choices that you are facing at this time in your life? Describe.

We are not alone in making choices. We can go to our ultimate source for guidance—our Lord and His Word. Jesus said, "But when he, the Spirit of truth, comes, he will guide you into all truth" (John 16:13). *Ned, SMTTP, Forefront*

How do you feel about basing your choices on following Jesus and leaving the consequences of your decisions to Him?   *Follow Jesus*

David's sin of counting his fighting men is recorded in 2 Samuel 24.
> The word of the Lord had come to Gad the prophet . . . "Go and tell David, 'This is what the Lord says: I am giving you three options. Choose one of them for me to carry out against you' " (vv 11-13).

None of the three options were good. "David said to Gad, 'I am in deep distress. Let us fall into the hands of the Lord, for his mercy is great; but do not let me fall in the hands of men' " (v 14).

Although David suffered consequences, he knew the importance of placing the consequences "into the hands of the Lord."

# Spiritual-Awareness

Jesus is interested in helping us make choices. He wants us to make choices that will bear good fruit in the present and the future. "If you remain in me and my words remain in you, ask whatever you wish, and it will be given you" (John 15:7).

*Ask, Abide*

Now let's look at biblical principles that can help us in making choices.

- **We are free to obey God in our choices.**

*Deuteronomy 28:1-2*
If the Israelites chose to fully obey the Lord, what consequences would follow?

- **We are free to disobey God in our choices.**

*Deuteronomy 28:15*
What would be the consequences if the Israelites disobeyed God?

- **Making right choices might bring suffering or even death, but it will bring God's eternal blessing.**

*Acts 7:54-60*
What consequences did Stephen receive for speaking the truth about God?

How do you picture heaven opening for Stephen?

- **We are responsible for the choices we make.**

*Deuteronomy 30:19-20*
What in these verses shows that we have the responsibility of *making choices*?

Session 7  Group Member's Guide: *Free to Grow*, Living Free, P. O. Box 22127, Chattanooga, TN 37422-2127

*Luke 15:11-20*
The prodigal son took personal responsibility for his return to his father.

What did he say in verses 18-20 that shows he made a responsible choice without blaming others or circumstances?

*Admitted he had sinned*

- We are free to make choices in family decisions that honor God.
  *Joshua 24:14-15*

What choice did Joshua make for himself and his household?

Is this a choice that you or someone in your household needs to make? Describe.

# Application

It is good to know that Jesus never changes. When you climbed out of bed this morning, regardless of how you might have felt, He had not changed during the night. "Jesus Christ is the same yesterday and today and forever" (Hebrews 13:8). He is trustworthy and consistent.

In facing choices, Proverbs 3:5-6 will help us bring God into the choices we make. "Trust in the LORD with all your heart and lean not on your own understanding; in all your ways acknowledge him, and he will make your paths straight" ("he shall direct thy paths" KJV).

Sandra Wilson in her book *Hurt People Hurt People* has an equation for change. She says,
   New choices + consistent practice = change (p. 87).

In order to be free to grow and to better honor God in our lifestyle and/or relationships, we sometimes need to make changes or adjustments.

In light of Wilson's *theory of change*, describe an area in which you need to change or adjust. *Do only what God has for me to do. The rest is part of life.*

It is all about your right to choice. You can choose to live in the past and feel about what may have happened to you or what you lost, or you can acknowledge your past and move on. You can never reach your future if you won't remove yourself from your past (Schlessinger, p. 11).

*[handwritten: Move on!]*

**New Choices:** What are your new choices?

*[handwritten: Declutter; Routine (healthy) Live for Jesus & others]*

**Consistent Practice:** What behaviors or attitudes will you consistently practice (or continue to practice)?

*[handwritten: Bit by bit put in order Pray, make known their value & gifts]*

**Change:** No matter how small, what changes are you observing in your life?

There is safety in godly accountability. "Where no counsel is, the people fall: but in the multitude of counsellors there is safety" (Proverb 11:14 KJV).

Who will you look to for godly accountability?

Remember, when we practice Proverbs 3:5-6 in making choices, God has room to work in our lives. God's plan for us as we make new choices will be to give us hope for the future. We can acknowledge the past hurt or pain but not wallow in it. We can move on with Jesus in control of our lives.

# Session 8: Freedom and Responsibility

**Personal Preparation: Getting Ready for Session Eight**

## Meet With God

**Personal Notes**

Take 30 minutes each day to be alone with God in meditation and prayer. Read Luke 15, Ephesians 3 and Philippians 2.

*Lost Sheep, Lost Coins*
*Prodigal Son*

*Holy Spirit strength*
*Shine as lights in the world*

What object, animal, person, bird, etc. most symbolizes freedom to you?

*Jesus*

## Self-Awareness

Freedom and responsibility can be described as a coin with freedom on one side and responsibility on the other side. In order for us to experience spiritual and emotional growth and live effective lives, we must be responsible for our decisions and actions to be *free to grow*. With freedom comes responsibility in how we use that freedom.

During a seminar, a young lady, obviously upset, spoke to me during a break. In a painful and angry state of mind, she questioned, "How can you suggest that I (although she had not been singled out) forgive my father who sexually abused me over and over again as a young child? I will never forgive him."

Showing understanding and concern, I empathized with her but also spoke the truth in love to her. I pointed out that her father was still controlling her life because of her unwillingness to forgive him. To forgive her father would mean taking the responsibility to forgive, and the consequence of her choice would be freedom.

Group Member's Guide: *Free to Grow*, Living Free, P. O. Box 22127, Chattanooga, TN 37422-2127

Within your comfort level, share a responsibility you need to take (or continue) in order to experience freedom in an area of your life.

Jesus says, "Then you will know the truth, and the truth will set you free" (John 8:32). John 8:31 shows the responsibility that needs to be taken for this freedom to be ours.

What is it?

Holding to Jesus' teaching is our responsibility. The teaching of Jesus will lead to salvation and freedom from the bondage of sin. "You must make a determined commitment to change and move forward confidently on that commitment. Let Jesus Christ take charge of your life and give you the direction and strength you need" (Wright, p. 76).

## Spiritual-Awareness

The Bible shows the balance of freedom and responsibility. It has a compelling message for freedom through the finished work of Christ on the cross and the numerous passages that show that we have a responsibility to be a disciple of Christ. The goal is maturity in our Lord and Savior.

- We are challenged to grow in Christ.

*2 Peter 3:18*
What are the two areas of growth in this passage?

*Grace & Knowledge of Jesus*

- Freedom is often found by acting responsibly outside our comfort zone.

*Genesis 12:1-2*
The Lord asked Abram to leave his country (that which was familiar to him—his comfort zone).

What would this act of faith lead to?

*Great nation & God's blessing*

- Freedom and responsibility go hand in hand.

*Deuteronomy 28:1-2*

Describe the freedom and responsibility found in these verses and how they relate to each other.

*Must obey for blessings*

*Luke 15:18-20*

Coming to our senses, waking up to our present state of mind and life situation, can lead us to take responsibility/ownership for irresponsible decisions.

What in verses 18-20 shows the prodigal son's willingness to take responsibility and humble himself before God and man?

*"I will go & confess sin to God."*

When the prodigal son returned home, there was a celebration (vv 22-24). He was now in a position to grow in God's grace because he had taken the steps to freedom by being responsible for his actions.

- Freedom and confidence often go hand in hand.

*Ephesians 3:12*

In this passage there is a responsibility that is followed by "freedom and confidence." *"In Him & through faith in Him"*

What are the responsibility and the subsequent freedom in this scripture?

*Faith in Him*

*Approach God*

# Application

Freedom is something we all want, but responsibility is the challenge that we must address to experience God's freedom. Working through the painful choices made in the past is not easy. Walking through the "threshold of pain" is difficult but necessary. Experiencing freedom to grow is usually a process and not an overnight quick fix. It will take time, tears, and an unwavering commitment to follow the truths of biblical principles that will change your life.

Moses knew about pain and disappointments, but he stayed the course. The same can be said about David, Daniel, Joseph, and others.

Jesus is there to help you each step of the way.
> God has said, "Never will I leave you; never will I forsake you." So we say with confidence, "The Lord is my helper; I will not be afraid. What can man do to me?" (Hebrews 13:5-6).

God has a part and we have a part in the process of becoming free to grow. Paul writes, "Continue to work out your salvation with fear and trembling, for it is God who works in you to will and to act according to his good purpose" (Philippians 2:12-13).

God works in us from the inside out. We work out our salvation by walking in obedience and accepting our responsibility.

Trusting God for freedom and confidence, list the area(s) where you are working or plan to work through pain to make changes (or you anticipate such) and to be more responsible. On this list make two columns. On one side put your part in the process of change and in the other column put God's part. Use the chart on page 45.

| My Responsibility | God's Responsibility |
|---|---|
| Day by Day Follow | He leads |
| Listen, Seek | Wisdom, Patience Given |
| Go to Him | Comfort, Peace |

Hebrews 4:10 encourages us to rest in God—"For anyone who enters God's rest also rests from his own work, just as God did from his."

# Session 9: Fresh Start

**Personal Preparation: Getting Ready for Session Nine**

## Meet With God

*Personal Notes*

Take 30 minutes each day to be alone with God in meditation and prayer. Read Lamentations 3, Romans 12, 2 Corinthians 10 and Job 42.

Briefly describe your week since we last met—your thoughts, actions, reflections, etc., as they relate to this *Free to Grow* small group.

*God is with me, providing what I need, forgiving and not condemning me for past decisions & actions. He loves me; I am His daughter seeking His way & resting in His peaceful arms.*

# Self-Awareness

Overcoming setbacks and disappointments of life will mean making a fresh start. For example, for some a fresh start means building a totally new foundation and life in Christ because of a destructive and disruptive past. A fresh start may mean a husband who needs more empathy and understanding in order to be more in tune with his wife's past setbacks. Without help, the wife's pain will eventually spill over into the entire family system.

> Those of us who were wounded in our childhood drag into marriage the same sack of problems and pain we carried as single adults. We may have been able to hide the baggage long enough to distract our spouse from noticing its size or power, but soon our wounds surface in our new marriage (Hegstron, pp. 87-88).

Whether we need to start over or just make an adjustment, the Lord provides us with a *fresh start* no matter what the setback or disappointment or how long you and/or your family have suffered from the pain.

Describe your need. Do you need to make a fresh start or make an adjustment in your personal life or family?

We must remember that making a fresh start is a process. Jesus is the "fresh journey" and that is because our life is "now hidden with Christ in God" (Colossians 3:3). This is how we find the ability to walk the process. Jesus said, "I am the way" (John 14:6). He enables us by his Holy Spirit to walk in new paths. This process has some pitfalls because of the *flesh*, but it is one of the joys as we experience the effectiveness of a fresh start in Christ.

Jeremiah was no stranger to being in God's will, yet he had his share of suffering. He suffered not for his poor choices but rather by the hands of his own people and the oppression of the Babylonians. God yearned for the Israelites to repent and make a fresh start.

Known as the weeping prophet, Jeremiah describes his deep suffering in the book of Lamentations. He shows that our God provides hope and newness (or freshness) for every day (Lamentations 3:21-23).

What hope for a fresh start do you find in these verses?

# Spiritual-Awareness

As we make our fresh start, the Bible assures us that God's Word is faithful and trustworthy for life's issues. "All Scripture is God-breathed and is useful for teaching, rebuking, correcting and training in righteousness, so that the man of God may be thoroughly equipped for every good work" (2 Timothy 3:16-17).

- A fresh start means a renewed mind.

*Romans 12:1-2*

In verse 2, what is our responsibility in order to have a renewed mind? *Know & approve what God's will is*

We are called to honor God. Anything we do that dishonors God in our relationships, attitudes, unforgiveness, bitterness, etc. is conforming to this world. As we honor God, a renewed mind will clean out the debris, junk, and impaired thinking.

- The mind is a battlefield where Satan attacks.

*2 Corinthians 10:3-6*

This passage describes the spiritual battle.

What is our responsibility in this battle?
*Truth*

Our battle is not against bad parents, spouses, etc. Paul writes, "Put on the full armor of God so that you can take your stand against the devil's schemes. For our struggle is not against flesh and blood" (Ephesians 6:11-12).

- A fresh start involves repentance.

*Ezekiel 18:30*

How can we prevent sin from disrupting our fresh start?

*Trust in the Lord! Always rely on Him!!*

- Through Christ, a fresh start involves every aspect of our life.

*2 Corinthians 5:17*

What does this verse say about anyone who is "in Christ?"

*new Creation*

This radical change is the experience of all who have received Christ as Savior. Whether you have just received Jesus Christ as your Savior or rededicated your life, a "new creation" (fresh start) means that you are a completely new creation, not in just one compartment of your life but in your entire being. His plan is to renew every area of your life. His plan is to renew every area of your life—your family, employment, lifestyle—everything is placed under His guidance and loving care.

Do you have a tendency to compartmentalize God, or is He involved in all facets of your life? Describe.

As we honor God in all areas of our life without compartmentalizing Him, we will experience a fresh start. As time goes on, the rearview mirror will show the setbacks, disappointments, and pain becoming less impactful. The scars will still remain but only as a reminder of God's grace.

## Application

It is comforting to know that we have God's approval and help in overcoming the setbacks and disappointments of life. Regardless of where you are in your growth, spiritually and emotionally, you are a candidate for a fresh start. This old saying remains true, "Today is the first day of the rest of your life."

God loves you just the way you are, but He loves you too much to leave you the way you are. If you choose to honor God in your fresh start, He will be with you every step of the journey.

H. Norman Wright asks a very important question, "Are you a yesterday person?" (p. 61). We can be free of past disappointments by focusing on Jesus and abiding in His Word. God is able and will help you. Paul writes, "Now to him who is able to do immeasurably more than all we ask or imagine, according to his power that is at work within us, to him be glory in the church and in Christ Jesus throughout all generations, for ever and ever! Amen" (Ephesians 3:20-21).

Job needed a fresh start. After he lost everything and experienced a lengthy time of despair and poor counsel from his friends, God gave him a fresh start.

God permitted Satan to attack him in a ruthless way (Job 1:12). In all his troubles Job remained faithful to God. During his despair, he penned these words, "I know that my Redeemer lives . . . And after my skin is destroyed, yet in my flesh I will see God" (Job 19:25-26).

Job 42:10 summarizes his fresh start. "After Job had prayed for his friends, the LORD made him prosperous again and gave him twice as much as he had before." It is interesting to note that this happened "after Job had prayed for his friends."

Who do you need to pray for today?

Write a prayer to God expressing your desire for or thanking Him for a fresh start. Thank Him because He has made you into a new creation. List the old that has gone and the new that has come into your life. In the struggles that you have entrusted to His care, thank Him that His grace is sufficient to help you.

# Session 10: Developing the Character of Christ

**Personal Preparation: Getting Ready for Session Ten**

## Meet With God

*Personal Notes*

Take 30 minutes each day to be alone with God in meditation and prayer. Read Galatians 5, Romans 8, and Psalm 1.

The *Webster's Student Dictionary* defines character as the "central being of a person which makes him/her an individual who is different from all others."

Name and describe a person you know and respect as one who stands out because of his/her character.

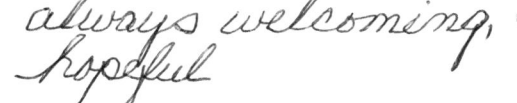

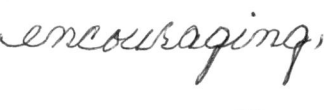

*always welcoming, encouraging, hopeful*

## Self-Awareness

Developing the character of Christ means giving up undeveloped character. We can choose to be led by the Spirit—a choice opposed by the sinful nature. Undeveloped character or sinful nature looks like this:

> It is obvious what kind of life develops out of trying to get your own way all the time: repetitive, loveless, cheap sex; a stinking accumulation of mental and emotional garbage; frenzied and joyless grabs for happiness; trinket gods; magic-show religion; paranoid loneliness; cutthroat competition; all-consuming-yet-never-satisfied wants; a brutal temper; an impotence to love or be loved; divided homes and divided lives; small-minded and lop-sided pursuits; the vicious habit of depersonalizing everyone into a rival; uncontrolled and uncontrollable addictions; ugly parodies of community. I could go on.
>
> This isn't the first time I have warned you, you know. If you use your freedom this way, you will not inherit God's kingdom (Galatians 5:19-21 THE MESSAGE).

Group Member's Guide: *Free to Grow*, Living Free, P. O. Box 22127, Chattanooga, TN 37422-2127

Can you see any undeveloped character traits in your life? Describe the area that causes you the most concern.

Unfortunately, "the acts of the sinful nature" (v19 NIV) are rather normal for the culture we live in today. When we choose to be led by God's Spirit, we will stand out in the crowd and can be a powerful witness for Christ.

"Those controlled by the sinful nature cannot please God" (Romans 8:8).

We do not have to live under the power of sin. "And if the Spirit of him who raised Jesus from the dead is living in you, he who raised Christ from the dead will also give life to your mortal bodies through his Spirit, who lives in you. Therefore, brothers, we have an obligation—but it is not to the sinful nature, to live according to it" (Romans 8:11-12).

According to Romans 8:13, how do we deal with the misdeeds of the body ("the sinful nature")? *by the Spirit put to death the deeds of the body*

## Spiritual-Awareness

To develop the character of Christ in our life is to develop the fruit of the Spirit in our personal life. "It is called the fruit of the Spirit because the Spirit is its source. It does not grow naturally out of the soil of our human flesh" (Gee, p. 42). Through the Holy Spirit, we can develop a plentiful harvest.

Now let's look at each of the fruit of the Spirit with the determination to develop the character of Christ in our life.

*Galatians 5:22-23*
- Love

1 Corinthians 13:4-7 describes God's love.
> Love is patient, love is kind. It does not envy, it does not boast, it is not proud. It is not rude, it is not self-seeking, it is not easily angered, it keeps no record of wrongs. Love does not delight in evil but rejoices with the truth. It always protects, always trusts, always hopes, always perseveres.

What stands out to you in this description of love?

The fruit of the Spirit begins with love, and all of the fruit is centered around love.

- Joy

How is joy expressed in Philippians 3:1?

*Rejoice in the Lord*

Active rejoicing is nurtured by the Spirit whether the outward circumstances are favorable or not.

What does Paul say about joy in Romans 15:13?

*God fills us with joy & peace when we believe. Then we have hope by the power of the Holy Spirit.*

- Peace

Describe from Philippians 4:7 the incredible *peace of God*.

*Surpasses understanding & guards your heart and mind through Christ Jesus.*

The peace of God is not man-made or based on favorable or unfavorable circumstances. This peace is from the Holy Spirit—a calm assurance that indicates that God is in control.

- Patience

This kind of long-suffering is found in Ephesians 4:2.

How can we be patient with those who may upset us or deliberately hurt us? *with lowliness & gentleness*

A patient person, empowered by the Holy Spirit, is not revengeful. This fruit leaves "room for God's wrath" (Romans 12:19).

- Kindness

Proverbs 15:1 shows the value of kindness.

What is one of the results of showing kindness? *turns away wrath by a soft answer*

- **Goodness**

Goodness is an indicator of character in a person's life. Goodness embodies dependability, generosity, and uprightness and shows goodness to others.

In 2 Peter 1:5-7, what quality precedes *goodness*? *faith*

Goodness (moral excellence) develops out of our faith in Christ.

- **Faithfulness**

Character is shown by our faithfulness and obedience to God. We must also demonstrate faithfulness in our responsibilities and in our relationships with people.

In 1 Corinthians 4:2, Paul indicates that those "who have been given a trust" must prove themselves.

How are they to prove themselves? *God is the judge*

- **Gentleness**

Gentleness is a combination of gentleness and kindness. It is directed toward people. As with the other fruit, it is empowered by the Holy Spirit in our lives.

In view of Philippians 4:5, how generous are we to be with our gentleness? *be gentle with all*

- **Self-Control**

The Lord helps us deal with the temptations of the flesh (desires, impulses, ungodly passions, lust). He helps us develop self-control to master these stumbling blocks as we surrender to the Spirit's guidance.

In 1 Corinthians 9:24-26, Paul compares this life to an athletic event. Verse 25 tells us what is necessary to compete in this game.

What does it require? *Run to obtain the prize (discipline)*

"You've all been to the stadium and seen the athletes race. Everyone runs; one wins. Run to win. All good athletes train hard. They do it for a gold medal that tarnishes and fades. You're after one that's gold eternally" (1 Corinthians 9:24-25 THE MESSAGE).

To develop the character of Christ in our life, we must make discipline an important part of our life. We are not alone; the Holy Spirit will help us.

# Application

The big question is, "How do I develop the character of Christ in my life?" By developing the fruit of the Spirit, I will develop the character of Christ. I do this by cooperating with the Holy Spirit. The fruit will need to be cultivated. This is a lifetime process. The secret is abiding in Him.

As we bear fruit, there will be times of pruning. Jesus says, "I am the true vine, and my father is the gardner. He cuts off every branch in me that bears no fruit, while every branch that does bear fruit he prunes so that it will be even more fruitful" (John 15:1-2).

In what ways are you responding to His pruning? Describe.

Psalm 1:1-3 describes safeguards which will protect the fruit in our lives and help us develop the character of Christ.

> Blessed is the man who does not walk in the counsel of the wicked or stand in the way of sinners or sit in the seat of mockers. But his delight is in the law of the LORD, and on his law he meditates day and night. He is like a tree planted by streams of water, which yields its fruit in season and whose leaf does not wither.

Notice the safeguards against the progression of sin. We should not
- Walk in the counsel of the wicked (act on/take the advice of)—ungodly counsel.
- Stand in the way of sinners (hang around with)—negative influences.
- Sit in the seat of mockers (dwell with, be comfortable with)—scorning others.

How are these safeguards applicable to relationships?

If you are living with a family member who could be described by one of the three preceding categories, how can you protect yourself from the ungodly influence?

How do you maintain a godly influence?
*meditate on His Word*

Character will show its true colors. "Make a tree good and its fruit will be good, or make a tree bad and its fruit will be bad, for a tree is recognized by its fruit" (Matthew 12:33).

Remember the *Webster's Student Dictionary* definition of character—the "central being of a person which makes him/her an individual who is different from all others." Be a difference maker for Jesus. Develop the character of Christ.

Write a prayer to God describing your needs in character development, your desire to be a difference maker for Jesus, and your need for His help in the process.

# Session 11: Developing Freedom in Christ

**Personal Preparation: Getting Ready for Session Eleven**

## Meet With God

**Personal Notes**

Take 30 minutes each day to be alone with God in meditation and prayer. Read Genesis 2-3, Luke 4, and John 8.

When did "freedom in Christ" become more than just words to you, and how did it happen?

## Self-Awareness

Free means to not be imprisoned or tied down. Freedom is the state of being free or living free. To be imprisoned means more than just being incarcerated in a prison or jail for a crime. Many people live in spacious and comfortable homes with all the perks, but they are still in prison. On the other hand, many people who are serving prison terms are experiencing *freedom in Christ* because they have a personal relationship with Jesus Christ.

Although he was not being held in a material, human prison, David prayed, "Set me free from my prison, that I may praise your name" (Psalm 142:7).

Are you experiencing freedom in Christ, or is there a certain area in your life that imprisons you?

How has this affected your willingness or desire to praise the Lord?

Group Member's Guide: *Free to Grow*, Living Free, P. O. Box 22127, Chattanooga, TN 37422-2127

God places a high value on freedom. From the very beginning, He gave us the freedom to choose good or evil, right or wrong, obedience or disobedience. We have the choice to be free or to live in bondage.

In Genesis 2:16-17, He gave a command. "You are free to eat from any tree in the garden; but you must not eat from the tree of the knowledge of good and evil, for when you eat of it you will surely die."

Genesis 3:6 shows how Eve used her freedom. What did she do?

*she ate*

Adam and Eve's choice to disobey God has affected the history of mankind. God sent His son Jesus Christ, who died on the cross of Calvary for our sins that we might be free in Christ.

John 10:10 describes why Jesus came to help us and the alternative Satan offers. *(steal, kill, destroy)* *Jesus: abundant life*

What does He say?

True freedom is in Christ. We have a certain destiny. Circumstances cannot confuse us as we remember we are made in the image of God and that God is in ultimate control.

## Spiritual-Awareness

Now let's turn to the book that proclaims the availability of liberty for all. "If you hold to my teaching, you are really my disciples. Then you will know the truth, and the truth will set you free" (John 8:31-32). In the Bible we can anchor to the truth that will forever bring the freedom of Christ into our lives, regardless of our past setbacks and disappointments.

- Jesus has come to bring freedom into your life.

Luke 4:18-19
In this passage, Jesus proclaims freedom spoken by the prophet Isaiah. What is the message? *God is in control*

In 2 Peter 1:4, we are invited to "participate in the divine nature." There is *now* a power within you—not in the sweet by-and-by but now.

- Jesus has the authority and willingness to set us free from the bondage of sin.

*John 8:36*
What happens when the Son sets you free?

John says, "To him who loves us and has freed us from our sins by his blood, and has made us to be a kingdom and priests to serve his God and Father—to him be glory and power for ever and ever! Amen" (Revelation 1:5-6).

- We are to use our "freedom in Christ" wisely.

*Galatians 5:13*
We were called to be free. But how are we to use our freedom wisely?

"You have been set free from sin and have become slaves to righteousness" (Romans 6:18).

- Freedom affects our giving of ourselves and our resources.

*Matthew 10:8*
What does this verse say about giving and receiving?

"But who am I, and who are my people, that we should be able to give as generously as this? Everything comes from you, and we have given you only what comes from your hand" (1 Chronicles 29:14).

# Application

Maintaining a daily walk in which we experience freedom in Christ is a process of growth in Him. We are called to be led by the Spirit of God and to deny sinful desires. Paul writes, "live by the Spirit, and you will not gratify the desires of the sinful nature" (Galatians 5:16).

Developing freedom in Christ calls for us to cooperate with the Holy Spirit. Paul also says in Galatians 5:25, "Since we live by the Spirit, let us keep in step with the Spirit."

Picture a precision-like marching band in your mind. Now relate that to the various areas of your life. Where do you see yourself—in step, out of step, in line, out of line? Describe.

As viewers can quickly see when a member of a precision marching band is out of step, Jesus as well as friends who love you will know when you are in or out of step. James writes, "Therefore confess your sins to each other and pray for each other so that you may be healed [in step with the band]. The prayer of a righteous man is powerful and effective" (James 5:16).

Another analogy for developing freedom in Christ is an athletic event. Paul writes, "You were running a good race. Who cut in on you and kept you from obeying the truth?" (Galatians 5:7). Paul was addressing Christians who were being led astray by well-meaning but unwise believers. Our enemy, Satan, still uses well-meaning people as well as many other devious means to cut in on our race of life and trip us up.

What are some of ways the enemy might try to cut in on you in this race? Describe.

Which of these have you experienced personally in your life?

Write a prayer to God expressing your sincere desire to develop a freedom in Christ that will overcome every obstacle of the past, present, and future. Mix in the precision marching band and athletic race comparisons as much as you can.

To give yourself a checkup on developing freedom in Christ, always be aware of Colossians 2:6-8:

> So then, just as you received Jesus Christ as Lord, continue to live in him, rooted and built up in him, strengthened in the faith as you were taught, and overflowing with thanksgiving. See to it that no one takes you captive through hollow and deceptive philosophy, which depends on human tradition and the basic principles of this world rather than on Christ.

*the solid rock I stand*

# Session 12: Developing a Future in Christ

**Personal Preparation: Getting Ready for Session Twelve**

## Meet With God

**Personal Notes**

Take 30 minutes each day to be alone with God in meditation and prayer. Read Esther 1-10 and Revelation 21..

What has been most meaningful to you in the group during our time together?

## Self-Awareness

Although this group, *Free to Grow,* is coming to a completion, our trust that we have been given a new nature and personal identity in Christ can continue and grow in the days, months, and years ahead. The character and freedom of Christ can become so much a familiar part of us that we almost forget the identity confusion we once lived with. Our purpose has been to create vision for and the reality of a new and growing life in which we overcome the setbacks and disappointments of life that gave us such an uncertain identity and lack of confidence. We have discovered together the deep roots of character, proclaiming and living in our freedom and celebrating the future we have in Christ. We have reason to look ahead with joy and excitement because Christ lives in us and is in charge of our future—both here on this earth and the life to come in heaven.

Let's go back to the verse in Jeremiah 29:11 that we discussed in earlier sessions.

> "For I know the plans I have for you," declares the LORD, "plans to prosper you and not to harm you, plans to give you hope and a future."

God promises us life now. The glory of God is a man or woman fully alive versus counting birthdays.

Looking forward into the future with this verse as the basis, describe your hopes for yourself.

In light of eternity, life here on earth is short. James describes life as "a mist that appears for a little while and then vanishes" (James 4:14).

Considering your short time on earth, what do you value most?
*relationships with God & others*

Heaven is the ultimate future for the believer.

During his earthly life, the Christian experiences by faith the presence of the invisible God; but in the life to come, this experience of faith will become an actual reality. He will see God face-to-face—a blessing described by some theologians as the Beatific Vision (Pearlman, p. 381).

From among those already in heaven, name some of your friends, family, and others you look forward to seeing in heaven.

Overcoming setbacks and disappointments needs to be acknowledged, but <u>we must move on in freedom to the future Christ has for us</u>. In Philippians 3:13-14, Paul discusses the past and the future.

Describe Paul's attitude regarding his past and his future.

*I press on to the goal to win the prize.*

## Spiritual-Awareness

As we walk this journey here on earth, the Scripture provides assurance that our Savior is going before us. He has already prepared a place for those who are "in Christ" in Heaven. Jesus comforts us with these words,

> Do not let your hearts be troubled. Trust in God; trust also in me. In my Father's house are many rooms; if it were not so, I would have told you. I am going there to prepare a place for you. And if I go and prepare a place for you, I will come back and take you to be with me that you also may be where I am (John 14:1-3).

- The love of God is with us.

*Romans 8:38-39*
What does Paul say about God's love regarding the present and the future?

*(Forget what is behind) Nothing can separate us from the love of God that is in Christ Jesus our Lord.*

What does this verse mean to you?

*He forgives; Jesus made a way.*

- God <u>provides guidance</u> for the future.

*Psalm 48:14*
What is the extent of God's guidance in this verse?

*Forever*

The Holy Spirit will provide guidance. Jesus said, "But when he, the Spirit of truth, comes, he will guide you into all truth" (John 16:13). <u>The Holy Spirit</u> came on the Day of Pentecost. <u>He is here to guide you day by day.</u>

- God promises us a heavenly body.

*2 Corinthians 5:1-5*
We know that when these bodies of ours are taken down like tents and folded away they will be <u>replaced by resurrection bodies in heaven</u>—<u>God-made, not handmade</u>—and we'll never have to relocate our "tents" again. Sometimes we can hardly wait to move—and so we cry out in frustration. Compared to what's coming, living conditions around here seem like a stopover in an unfurnished shack, and we're tired of it! We've been given a glimpse of the real thing, our true home, our resurrection bodies! The Spirit of God whets our appetite by giving us a taste of what's ahead. He puts a little of heaven in our hearts so that we'll never settle for less (THE MESSAGE).

In your own words, relate your thoughts on this passage. What is the most unforgettable part of this passage for you?

- Christ's return for His church brings encouragement.

*1 Thessalonians 4:16-18*
In these verses, we see how we should speak to each other about the coming of the Lord. What is Paul's advice?

*Encourage one another*

- A peaceful person has a future.

*Psalm 37:37-38*
What is available to the man of peace?

*future*

What about the future of the wicked?

God provides direction through the peace of Christ. "Let the peace of Christ rule [direct, lead, umpire] in your hearts" (Colossians 3:15). Submit to the peace of Christ. He will lead you in the present and future.

- Heaven will be a place of joy.

*Revelation 21:3-4*
According to verse 3, where will God dwell?
*among His people*

What does verse 4 say about sorrow in heaven?
*won't be any*

What is the number one sorrow you are looking forward to leaving behind on this earth?

It will be a joy to see Jesus in heaven. "But we know that when he appears, we shall be like him, for we shall see him as he is" (1 John 3:2).

## Application

We turn to the book of Esther to show how each of us can be a "difference maker" (in the present and the future) when led by God's plan for our life. Esther was in her youth when she was among other Jews "carried into exile from Jerusalem by Nebuchadnezzar king of Babylon, among those taken captive with Jehoiachin king of Judah. Mordecai had a cousin named Hadassah, whom he had brought up because she had neither father nor mother. This girl, who was also known as Esther, was lovely in form and features, and Mordecai had taken her as his own daughter when her father and mother died" (Esther 2:6-7).

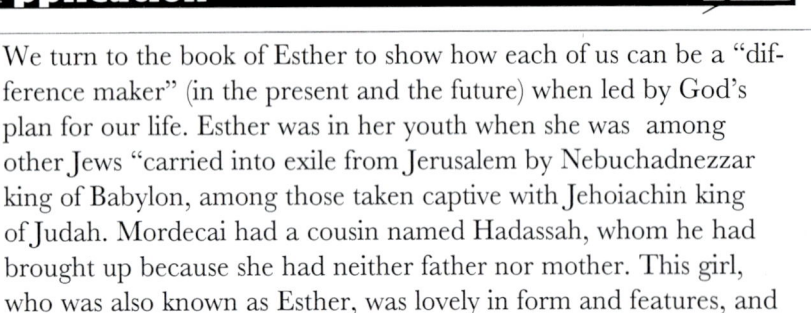

Since she was a young Jewish girl, Esther was no stranger to rejection. She also knew the pain of not having a father and mother.

Esther was an orphan, but her cousin, Mordecai, watched over her with loving care. He provided righteous counsel as she rose to the prominent position of queen.

To summarize her life, she took the place of the obstinate Queen Vashti and reigned beside King Xerxes and served as his queen.

Xerxes' top official was Haman. Haman became enraged because Mordecai would not bow down to him and thus claimed that all Jews were subversive. He devised a plan to annihilate all the Jews.

Mordecai requested that Esther risk her life and go before the king without an invitation and plead for the deliverance of the Jewish people from Haman's plan.

The king allowed Esther to speak, and God intervened through her to save the Jewish race from impending annihilation.

Now let's look at four major principles in Esther's life that we can incorporate into our present and future life.

- Always be ready for the unique opportunity the Lord may place in your life.

Esther's rise to the queenship of Persia was not an accident or a coincidence. Someone has defined coincidences as "miracles in which God prefers to remain anonymous" (Gilbrant, p. 295).

When Esther had the opportunity to make a difference, Mordecai said, "For if you remain silent at this time, relief and deliverance for the Jews will arise from another place" (Esther 4:14).

Do you feel confident the Lord is prompting you to act, pray, assist, or plan in a certain situation? Describe.

Have you remained silent and failed to act on this opportunity? Describe.

As believers, let us remember that God is working in what happens around us. "If God is for us, who can be against us?" (Romans 8:31).

- The timing of God is very important in our lives.

Mordecai said, "Who knows but that you have come to royal position for such a time as this?" (Esther 4:14).

Have you considered that God might have you in a place or situation in your life "for such a time as this"?

"Every child of God is where God has placed him for some purpose, and the practical use of this . . . point is to lead you to inquire, for what practical purpose has God placed each one of you where you now are?" (Spurgeon, p. 401).

Let us keep in mind this verse which we have discussed in a previous session: "Since we live by the Spirit, let us keep in step with the Spirit" (Galatians 5:25).

- Our future with God may involve risk.

"Then Esther sent this reply to Mordecai: 'Go, gather together all the Jews who are in Susa, and fast for me. Do not eat or drink for three days, night or day. I and my maids will fast as you do. When this is done, I will go to the king, even though it is against the law. And if I perish, I perish' " (Esther 4:15-16).

What was Esther's request?

What did Esther say about the risk involved?

As she awaited her fate, "On the third day Esther put on her royal robes and stood in the inner court of the palace, in front of the king's hall" (Esther 5:1). She did not know if she had minutes to live or if execution awaited her. However, she was willing to take the risk for her people.

- Like Esther, we need to be a people of character—she was prepared for the present and future.

Esther was not prideful. She was willing to receive the righteous council from Mordecai. She was not ashamed of her racial or spiritual heritage.

It was in the plan of God to use Esther to preserve the Jewish race at this time. Although she became nothing less than a spiritual giant, her attitude was consistent. Her character was deeply rooted in God—she could be trusted for such a task.

Write a prayer to God thanking Him for helping you during *Free to Grow*. Ask Him to guide you with the proper attitude to deal with friends, family, and others who do not understand your change. Pray for a humble spirit. Also describe in your prayer the attitude you want to display to others. Use Esther as a guide for your prayer. Ask God for a plan for continued growth through a small group, counseling, fellowship with believers, etc. Acknowledge your need for accountability. "Commit to the LORD whatever you do, and your plans will succeed" (Proverbs 16:3).

# Resources

## Is there any good reason why you cannot receive Jesus Christ right now?

**How to receive Christ:**

1. Admit your need (that you are a sinner).

2. Be willing to turn from your sins (repent).

3. Believe that Jesus Christ died for you on the cross and rose from the grave.

4. Through prayer, invite Jesus Christ to come in and control your life through the Holy Spirit (receive Him as Savior and Lord).

---

**What to Pray**

Dear God,
I know that I am a sinner and need Your forgiveness.
I believe that Jesus Christ died for my sins.
I am willing to turn from my sins.
I now invite Jesus Christ to come into my heart and life as my personal Savior.
I am willing, by God's strength, to follow and obey Jesus Christ as the Lord of my life.

_____
Date          Signature

---

The Bible says: "Everyone who calls on the name of the Lord will be saved" (Romans 10:13).

"Yet to all who received him, to those who believed in his name, he gave the right to become children of God" (John 1:12).

"Therefore, since we have been justified through faith, we have peace with God through our Lord Jesus Christ" (Romans 5:1).

When we receive Christ, we are born into the family of God through the supernatural work of the Holy Spirit who lives within every believer. This process is called regeneration or the new birth.

Share your decision to receive Christ with another person.

Connect to a local church.

Group Member's Guide: *Free to Grow*, Living Free, P. O. Box 22127, Chattanooga, TN 37422-2127

# Quotes and References

Augsburger, David. *The Freedom of Forgiveness*. Chicago: Moody Press, 1977.

Boice, James Montgomery. *Psalms—Volume I*. Grand Rapids: Baker Books, 1994.

Brand, Paul, and Phillip Yancy. *In His Image*. Grand Rapids: Zondervan Publishing House, 1987.

Crabb, Lawrence J. *Understanding People*. Grand Rapids: Zondervan, 1987.

Gee, Donald. *A New Discovery*. Springfield, Missouri: Gospel Publishing House, 1932.

Gilbrant, Thoraf, and Gregory A. Lint. *The Complete Biblical Library—Ezra, Nehemiah, Esther, Job*. Springfield, Missouri: World Library Press, 2000.

Harris, Ralph W., Stanley M. Horton, and Gayle Garrity Seaver. *The Complete Biblical Library—Romans, Corinthians*. Springfield, Missouri: World Library Press, 1989.

Hegstrom, Paul. *Broken Children, Grown-Up Pain*. Kansas City, Missouri: Beacon Hill Press, 2001.

Horton, Stanley M. *What the Bible Says About the Holy Spirit*. Springfield, Missouri: Gospel Publishing House, 1976.

Icenogle, Gareth Weldon. *Biblical Foundations for Small Groups*. Downers Grove, Illinois: InterVarsity Press, 1994.

Lawson, Ernie. *What I Practice, I Become*. Saint Paul, Minnesota: International Marriage Encounter, 1986.

Lee, Jimmy R. *The Ten Commandments*, Chattanooga, Tennessee: Living Free, 1998.

_____. *Understanding the Times*, Chattanooga, Tennessee: Living Free, 1997.

Lewis, C. S. *Mere Christianity*. New York: Macmillian, 1952.

Lewis, Thomas, Fari Amini, and Richard Lannon. *A General Theory of Love*. New York: Random House, Inc., 2001.

Pearlman, Myer. *Knowing the Doctrines of the Bible*. Springfield, Missouri: Gospel Publishing House, 1937.

Sande, Ken. *The Peacemaker*. Grand Rapids: Baker Books, 2004.

Schlessinger, Laura. *Bad Childhood—Good Life*. New York: HarperCollins, 2006.

Seamands, David. *Putting Away Childish Things*. Wheaton, Illinois: Victor Books, 1982.

Spurgeon, Charles H. *Men and Women of the Old Testament*. London: AMG Publishers, 1995.

Thrall, Bill, Bruce McNicol, and John Lynch. *True Faced*. Colorado Springs: NavPress, 2003.

Welch, Ed. "Who Are We? Needs, Longings, and the Image of God in Man." *The Journal of Biblical Counseling*, Volume 13, Number 1 (Fall 1994): 29.

Wilson, Sandra D. *Hurt People Hurt People*. Grand Rapids: Discovery House Publishers, 2001.

Wright, H. Norman. *Chosen for Blessing*. Eugene, Oregon: Harvest House, 1992.

# Notes

# Notes

# Notes